Someone I Love Has Died

Everyone Grieves
AND
No One Grieves Like Me!

Karen Lindwall-Bourg, LPC-S, Fellow Thanatologist

Emily Weyel, Illustrator

With Foreword by
Matthew Lindwall

Someone I Love Has Died: Everyone Grieves AND
No One Grieves Like Me © 2017 by Karen Lindwall-Bourg.
All Rights Reserved. No part of this publication may be reproduced, stored in a retrieval system, or transmitted in any form or by any means, electronic, mechanical, recording, or otherwise, without the prior written permission of the individual author or the publisher.

Published by
RHEMA Publishing House.™
rhemapublishinghouse.com
PO Box 1244 McKinney, TX 75070

For information about special discounts available for bulk purchases, sales promotions, and educational needs, contact RHEMA Publishing House at the above address.

This book is not intended as a substitute for the medical advice of physicians. The reader should consult a physician in matters related to his/her health and particularly with respect to any symptoms that may require diagnosis or medical attention. The author assumes no responsibility for any reader's attempts to self-diagnose any medical condition.

Scripture quotations are from the ESV® Bible (The Holy Bible, English Standard Version®), copyright © 2001 by Crossway, a publishing ministry of Good News Publishers. Used by permission. All rights reserved.

ISBN: 978-0-9983064-0-7
eBook ISBN: 978-0-9983064-3-8

Cover Design: Janie Owen-Bugh

Dedicated to
my grieving children,
Matthew, Melanie & Andrew—the M&Ms

Written for grieving children, ages 3-99,
and for those who walk this journey with them.

Table of Contents

Foreword by Matthew Lindwall

Introducing the Helping Grieving Children Series by RHEMA Publishing House 1

Other Titles in the Series 3

How to Use these Booklets: A Special Note to Those Working with Grieving Children 6

Someone I Love Has Died: Everyone Grieves AND No One Grieves Like Me 9

PART 1 12
  Everyone Grieves: Grief is Universal 12
  Everyone Grieves When Someone Dies 15
  Almost Everyone Grieves Other Losses as Well 20
  Sometimes People Grieve When Changes are Good 24

PART 2 27
  No One Grieves Just Like You Do: Grief is Unique........... 27
  The Whole Team Grieves Differently 31

Exercise: Try This! 35

About the Author 36

About the Illustrator 37

About Journey of Hope Grief Support Centers 38

Endnotes 39

Foreword

Every journey starts somewhere.

If you were to eventually become a mathematician, you couldn't start by learning calculus. There are so many steps before that. So in the same way, it's important to start your journey of grief and mourning at the beginning, and that means understanding that how you grieve is okay, even if it's different from the way others do it. I know that can be difficult to believe.

We live in a world where everyone is expected to play baseball to the same rules, to cross the road at certain points (the same way and together), and walk and talk and dress similarly. But grief isn't a game, and it's not as simple as crossing the street.

I remember going through this many times in my life, and it has always been hard for me to let myself grieve my way. Sometimes I even forget to consider what I really want and feel because I'm either concerned for someone else close to me who is also grieving, or because I'm afraid of what my grieving will look like to others.

But the hardest part for me is always what comes after I come to this understanding— that it's okay for me to grieve my way. The hardest part for me is helping others understand this as well. Most people in our lives are scared of grief, too, and some of them won't want to deal with their grief, much less yours. Many have an idea in their heads of how grief should be, and they may be hurtful with you because your way of grieving doesn't fit that picture in their heads. The hardest part is being a teacher to those around us while we're grieving.

I'll always remember that I'm in charge of how I grieve, and you should, too. You should know that it's important to grieve and mourn, and none of us can afford to bottle it up or pretend like we're not hurting when we are.

I encourage those who read this book to be brave and grieve boldly. Let it happen, and you may be surprised to find that your bravery inspires others to heal through grieving their way, too.

Matthew Lindwall

Introducing the "Helping Grieving Children" Series by RHEMA Publishing House

Walking alongside children and their caregivers who have experienced the devastating loss of a loved one is a special privilege! Knowing that we can help them to grieve well and work through and reconcile that loss in a way that brings healing and strength—as part of their new self and "new normal"—just makes life worth living!

- 1 in 5 children experience the death of someone close to them by age 18.[1]
- Studies from various countries on childhood bereavement following parental death report that children in this situation do experience a wide range of emotional and behavioral symptoms. The child often experiences an increase in anxiety with a focus on concerns about further loss, the safety of other family members, and fears around separation.[2]
- 7 in 10 classroom teachers (69%) currently have at least one student in their class(es) who has lost a parent, guardian, or close friend in the past year. They report that students who have lost a parent or guardian typically exhibit:
    - difficulty concentrating in class;
    - withdrawal or disengagement and less class participation;

- absenteeism;
- decrease in quality of work; and
- less reliability in turning in assignments[3]

The featured mini-booklets in the "Helping Grieving Children Series" were written for children everywhere who struggle to work through the myriad emotions felt and behaviors exhibited after losing a loved one.

Other Titles in the Series:

1. Someone I Love Has Died: Everyone Grieves AND No One Grieves Like Me! was written to describe grief as universal, and yet, so very unique to each person. Everybody grieves after the death of someone close, but one individual's pain and sorrow isn't ever "better" or "worse" than another's.

2. Someone I Love Has Died: Now Get Me OFF This Emotional Roller-Coaster Called GRIEF! describes life as FILLED with crazy twists and turns, scary ups and downs, unpredictable, and sometimes very hard times—like a roller-coaster— especially after someone you love has died. You will be okay, you will survive, and you may just come out a hero!

3. Someone I Love Has Died: Now What do I DO? encourages helpers and children to attend to the 7 tasks of embracing emotions and reconciling mourning.

4. Someone I Love Has Died: Grief is a Journey of Discovery The steps of grief and mourning are like going on a difficult journey, and the path you take and your final destination may look quite different than what you imagined. Through it all, you can keep going—and you will!

5. Someone I Love Has Died: Traditions & Rituals & Services, OH MY! Everyone is gathering around and talking about going to funerals and memorial services and activities! Let's talk about what's going on before, during, and after these services and the part you can take throughout the visits and services.

6. Someone I Love Has Died: Was it My Fault? Many times, after someone you love gets hurt or dies, you will often have thoughts that it might have been your fault: "If only I had___!" But it is NOT your fault that someone you love has died. Let me tell you how I know this is true!

7. Someone I Love Has Died: Why Can't I Meet My New Brother or Sister? explains miscarriage and stillbirth and how to help children understand what happens when a baby is lost in the womb and how to grieve that loss.

You can find more titles in the Helping Grieving Children Series at
http://rhemapublishinghouse.com/helping-grieving-children/

How to Use These Booklets

Dear Helping Professional and Parent/Guardian of grieving children,

Thank you for your efforts on behalf of hurting kids where you are. You are making a huge difference as a companion to bereaved children, walking alongside them while giving them the freedom to listen or talk or feel.

These booklets are divided into **parts and subsections** to make it easier for you to work through smaller sections at a time, especially with younger children.

Read slowly through this booklet series with your children. Stop and take time to let them chat about what they are learning. Work through the questions and activities in ways that incorporate all "six" senses—hearing, sight, touch, smell, and taste—-and I always add "heart"![4] We are to protect our hearts (the spring of life) with care, and to rest in the knowledge that "The Lord is near to the brokenhearted and saves the crushed in spirit." Psalm 34:18

Assure the children that you are there for them. Always be honest.

As you read, encourage children to attend to the ***7 Tasks of Embracing Emotions and Reconciling Mourning.***

Children need to

1. **acknowledge the reality of the death** as they confront the reality that someone they love has died and will not return. Help them work through their journey of grief, and gently talk about the fact that someone has died.
2. **embrace the pain of the death** while being nurtured physically, emotionally and spiritually. Listen to the children, and encourage the expression of thoughts and feelings. Allow them the freedom to experience their grief in manageable spurts and to relieve their pain through common play activities.
3. **remember the one who died.** Allow children to participate in all funeral and memorial activities to recall and share dreams and stories that mirror the significance of their relationship.
4. **develop a new self-identity based on a life without the person who died** that includes redefining their roles in the family and understanding that everyone dies. Help them see themselves uniquely through the perception or mirror of the one who died.

5. **relate the experience of the death to a context of new meaning** as they learn to appreciate life, look for goodness, explore their beliefs about life and death and grief and mourning. Help them by asking "how" and "why" questions, and allow them to grapple with some questions that have no answers.
6. **receive on-going support during the long process of mourning** that patiently allows them to grieve and offers a sensitive listening ear.[5]
7. **reconcile this loss as part of their life story.** Grieving the death of a loved one is not something people "get over" or from which they are cured. Grief is multi-faceted and each journey is unique. As part of their journey, families must learn to live with loss and the realization that life will never be the same. Over time they will gain a renewed sense of energy, confidence, and a desire to become re-involved in activities and to enjoy life again. Eating and sleeping and study and work habits will begin to return to normal as they regain the ability to concentrate. Family members will eventually establish new and healthy relationships. <u>This loss is reconciled and becomes a gentle companion and an integral part of LIFE</u>, and we begin to enjoy and see life more deeply and profoundly.[6]

Someone I Love Has Died

Everyone Grieves
AND
No One Grieves Like Me!

What is grief supposed to look like?

Years ago a popular commercial promoted a dog food brand with a catchy little jingle. It went something like this:
*"My dog's better than your dog,
My dog's better than yours,
My dog's better 'cause he eats Kennel Ration,
My dog's better than yours!"*

Well, it was a catchy tune! You can probably find it on the Internet to this very day!

But one person's pain and sorrow isn't ever **better** or **worse** than another's.

Everybody grieves when a close friend or relative dies. Grief may look the same sometimes; most people cry, are moody and grumpy, feel tired, can't stop thinking about the one who died, and more.

But not everyone grieves the same way—and that's OK! So grief may not look the same at all sometimes. One person may not seem to be sad—ever; another may be sad all day long and for many days in a row. One person may take care of others by preparing food and watching over her little brother or sister; and another may not be able to take care of himself or even tie his own shoelaces!

That's just the way grief looks sometimes.

And that's OK!

PART 1

Everyone Grieves: Grief is Universal

Grief is the internal experience of loss—all the big thoughts and feelings you experience within yourself after someone special dies. Mourning is the outward expression of grief—talking about the person who died, celebrating memories and anniversary dates, and showing others our emotions like crying, angry feelings, etc.

Almost everyone grieves and mourns after someone he or she loves dies. Sometimes grief looks the same all over the world.

Everyone grieves, you say?

Even God grieves! The Bible talks often about God being "grieved."[7] If He mourns, then we can be sure He understands when we are sad, and He has compassion for us.

God created us in His own image! Like Him!

"So God created man in his own image, in the image of God He created him; male and female He created them." Genesis 1:27

In Psalm 33, He tells us He "fashioned our hearts"! He made mankind similar in many ways and different from animals and plants.

So He created us and knows we grieve when someone we love dies, when we go through difficult changes in life. And He mourns with us!

Everyone Grieves When Someone Dies

Olivia's teacher had cancer and died right in the middle of the school year. Olivia isn't even sure she's supposed to be sad. She cries a lot, and she cries at the weirdest times! Sometimes she's so embarrassed; other times she wishes someone would notice her crying and come to comfort her.

Liam is moody and grumpy. Ever since his Dad died, one minute he wants to run outside to play and be with friends; another minute he just wants to be still and to be left alone. Sometimes he feels very sad; other times he doesn't feel anything at all! Sometimes he feels angry. Other times he feels guilty. It's so confusing.
He also feels like Olivia does sometimes.

Isabela still can't believe this terrible thing has happened. She wakes up and expects to see her Nana and hear her telling funny stories once more; then she remembers she died and it hurts all over again. She wants this to be a dream, so she pretends that Nana is traveling and will come back at any moment.

She also feels like Liam does sometimes.

Mason can't seem to finish his work at school or his chores at home. His cousin was in an accident and died. One minute Mason starts cleaning his room, and an hour later he looks up and discovers that he stopped working a long time ago. Sometimes he starts to tell someone something important, then he can't even remember what he wanted to say.

He also feels like Isabela does sometimes.

Emily misses her Mom so much. Her throat hurts all the time. She is having lots of headaches and stomachaches. She doesn't want to eat and she sleeps a lot, but she still feels really, really tired. She is having dreams—sometimes good dreams, sometimes bad ones. She's afraid it might have been her fault. Will this ever stop?

She also feels like Mason does sometimes.

Logan thinks about and wants to talk about his uncle all day long. He wants people to tell him the story of Uncle Dan's car accident over and over and over. Most people don't want to talk about it with him. He wants to be like his Uncle Dan and tries to walk and talk like he did.

He also feels like Emily does sometimes.

Riley feels uncomfortable around other people. She doesn't know what to say or do. She feels all alone. She can't decide if she wants other people to talk to her about her baby sister who died soon after being born or if she wants everyone to go about their business like nothing ever happened—like there was no baby at all.

She also feels like Logan does sometimes.

Almost everyone feels like these kids do at some time when someone he or she loves has died.

That's just the way grief looks sometimes.

Has someone you love died? Who was that person and what happened? In what ways have you felt like Olivia or Liam or Isabel or Mason or Emily or Logan or Riley?

Almost everyone grieves and mourns other losses and changes in their lives as well.

Oliver's dog Ranger, died. He was getting old and had been Oliver's best friend forever. They played and did everything together! Everyone acts like Ranger was "just a pet" and not his real pal. Oliver's not sure he ever wants another dog now.

Chloe' can't believe that her house burned down. Everything in it is gone—her toy dollhouse, her favorite books, her red rocking chair, her video games—all gone. She's wondering where they will sleep now, and she's afraid it might happen again. She's almost positive she can never be happy in another home. She doesn't want to live anywhere else!
She also feels like Oliver does sometimes.

Michael isn't sure whether he should be sad at all. He didn't even know his Dad's boss. But he knows his Dad is really struggling with a lot of emotions—he misses his boss. Michael at

least feels sad for his Dad and hates to see him worry about what it will be like at work now.
He also feels like Chloe' does sometimes.

Ronny's parents got divorced last year. He was so angry at his mom and dad! He had to move some of his toys to his house with his mom and some stayed at his house with his dad. Then his dad moved to a different city, and now Ronny only sees his dad once or twice a year. No one even asked him how he felt, and he's not sure if he's still angry or just sad that everything is different now.
He also feels like Michael does sometimes.

Everyone experiences losses and changes in life at some point and struggles with adjusting and with fears and with confusion. Big feelings and fears are often hard to understand.

That's just the way grief looks sometimes.

Have you experienced other losses too? What are some other things that might happen that will cause you to grieve or mourn? What has happened to you? In what ways have you felt like Oliver or Chloe' or Michael or Ronny?

Almost everyone experiences sadness and pain, even when changes in life are good!

Layla's step-dad got a new job, and her family moved somewhat far away from their old house and her friends and all that she was comfortable with. She's going to miss her school and church and the park that had a neat prairie dog pen in the middle where she and her friends would play. But she already has a new friend right across the street! Her name is Harper, and she introduced Layla to a really nice teacher and promises to show her around the neighborhood. And they both love to paint! She'll miss the old places where she used to play, but now they live so much closer to Papa Fred! That's cool, too!

Caleb's big brother got married last year. They don't get to live in the same house or spend as much time together anymore. That makes him sad. But now he has a new sister-in-law and she is really nice. She calls him her "brother," or sometimes she calls him her "bother-in-love." He never had a sister, so this is fun!

He also feels like Layla does sometimes.

Andrew's Mom just bought a new mini-van. It smells great and is his favorite color—blue! She says it is newer and safer, and that's a good thing. But it's not the same as the big van they used to have. He could stretch his legs much farther, and he claimed the back seat all to himself. He misses that van!

He also feels like Caleb does sometimes.

Just because some changes are good doesn't mean they won't be hard to deal with at times.

That's just the way grief looks sometimes.

What are some good changes that have happened to you? What has been good and hard about those changes? In what ways have you felt like Layla or Caleb or Andrew?

PART 2

No One Grieves Just Like You Do: Grief is Unique

What does it mean that grief is unique? If something is unique it is the only one of its kind!

You are one of a kind.
Your grief is the only one of its kind.

Knowing that God created us with lots of similarities and in His image, and that He grieves too, is comforting. But it is also comforting to know that He made us very unique. For example, I heard somewhere that if you took our DNA code and tried to map it and put it on paper, it would take over 200,000 pieces of paper—and that is in small print! Put it in a book, and the book would be over 16 feet tall!

And unless you are an identical twin, no two DNA codes are exactly the same. God understands both the sameness of grief and the uniqueness of grief.[8]

So, no other person's experience with death or loss is just like yours. You are one of a kind, so your journey of grief will be different from someone else's, even if they experienced the same death you did. You react to this loss in your own way

- because of the special person you are;
- based on who the person who died was, how they were related to you, and what they meant to you;
- depending on how it all happened;
- depending on how you are influenced by other losses you have experienced;
- especially if you're helped by those who are close to you who love you and are there for you.

You may experience several or only a few of the feelings that we've talked about so far. And you are surely able to tell us about many other physical feelings and emotions and actions of your own.

There is no right way to grieve and no set order of steps to take on this journey. Often, reactions are harder and happen more often right after a loss.

They usually become easier and happen less often over time.

This is your journey.

This is your grief.

It's up to you!

The Whole Team Grieves Differently

Evelyn and Adelyn are twins. Their friend Jayce was on their swim team that met after school for two years. Then he began to miss practices and meets, and after spending many nights in the hospital in another town, he died.

In some ways, they are suffering the same. In other ways, they and their teammates—Luke, Ryan, Arianna, Nora, Gabriel and Nicholas and their coach—are all grieving differently.

Evelyn and Adelyn both cry a little. Evelyn thinks she cries more. She is tired and isn't eating or sleeping, but Adelyn seems to be fine. She has lots of energy and sometimes finishes Evelyn's meals for her! They both have lots of dreams about Jayce. Evelyn has scary nightmares. Adelyn's dreams are all about the great times they had as teammates.

Luke and Ryan are on the team, too. Luke says he feels numb; he feels nothing and he doesn't want to talk about Jayce. Ryan says he feels everything all at once, and he feels strongly about everything that happened. He wants to talk about Jayce every time the team gets together.

Grief sometimes looks different for each person.

That's just the way grief looks sometimes.

Arianna and Nora are on the team. They both feel sad and are having trouble thinking clearly. They miss Jayce. Arianna is afraid of getting hurt. She's almost afraid of the water now! She wants everyone to be really careful while they practice, and she almost panics when they try new dives. She keeps warning everyone to be as safe as possible. Especially Nora! Nora seems to be taking lots of risks; she is fearless! She'll try anything new, and she isn't being careful. Yikes!

Gabriel and Nicholas are on the team. They both feel tired and restless at the same time.

Gabriel is mad and keeps getting in trouble at school and at home and on the team for acting out. Nicholas never gets in trouble at all. He has lost interest in school and isn't even sure he wants to stay on the team; he might quit and the team needs him! He says he feels guilty. He feels like Jayce's death was his fault somehow.

Coach Smith is having trouble thinking and focusing like everyone else. He's trying to hold it together for the team. But he's cross and touchy. They never know what might make him upset. He used to be the best coach! The whole team went to talk to the school counselor, but Coach Smith won't go.

Grief sometimes looks different for each person.

That's just the way grief looks sometimes.

Exercise
TRY THIS!

1. Ask someone in your life, who is a good listener, to listen to your whole story from start to finish about someone you love who has died.

2. Think of three really creative ways to let your family know when you feel like talking about your feelings and when you don't!

3. Pay it Forward: ask your family members or friends who are grieving if they want you to listen to their stories about someone they know who has died or about a big change in their lives.

About Karen Lindwall-Bourg

When Karen's husband Tim died in 1993, she and her 3 children (Matthew age 7, Melanie age 6, and Andrew age 4) attended The W.A.R.M. Place in Ft. Worth, TX for grief support. She met Fred, whose wife Cathy also died in 1993, and they had 3 children (Jon age 19, Lauren age 17, and Jeff age 14). Karen and Fred married, and their blended family has served in grief support centers for children since 1995.

Karen was the Program Director for Journey of Hope Grief Support Center, and her passion is to serve the Lord diligently by helping grieving families.

She is the Owner of and Counseling Supervisor at *RHEMA Counseling Associates*, a Biblical counseling training and grief support center headquartered in McKinney, TX, with satellite offices in Dallas and Mesquite that serve surrounding counties. You can learn more about Karen and RHEMA Associates at http://rhemacounseling.com.

RHEMA Counseling Associates now partners with and offers individual, couple, and family counseling at The Lighthouse for New Hope Center for Grief and Loss in Mesquite, TX. Their website is http://www.lighthousefornewhope.org/

Karen owns RHEMA Publishing House.

About Emily Weyel

Emily is a young teen and is my great niece! She's the second-born child in a thriving family with seven children and some really amazing parents. Because my husband Fred and I are both widowed and remarried, our blended and very extended families have added great variety and joy to our lives! Emily is part of these blended families. Every time we've been together I've been impressed with her strong faith, her maturity, her talents, and her gracious willingness to help with her large family.

Emily ~ Thank you so very much for your willingness to participate in the Helping Grieving Children Series of booklets. Thank you for your attention to detail and your diligence in finishing! May God richly bless you! It is my prayer that we can continue to work together for many years to come.

Blessings,

Aunt Karen

About *Journey of Hope Grief Support Center*

The first booklets in the "Helping Grieving Children" Series were written for the Journey of Hope Grief Support Center in Plano, TX to encourage children of all ages and those who seek to serve them to grieve well and live abundant lives.

Journey of Hope was established in 1997 as a non-profit organization dedicated to providing group grief support to children, adolescents, and their parents or adult caregivers who have lost a loved one to death. Journey of Hope offers these services in a warm, caring, and nurturing environment where the feelings of grief, pain, and loss may be expressed. Trained volunteer group facilitators lead participants in their personal journey toward healing and healthy reconciliation of their grief. You can learn more about them at http://johgriefsupport.org.

You can find children's grief support centers by searching at http://www.dougy.org/grief-support-programs/. This listing includes over 500 centers that provide grief support and services. It is our collective desire to share these resources with grieving children in Collin and surrounding counties and all over the world!

Endnotes

1. Kenneth Doka, ed., *OMEGA, Journal of Death and Dying*, www.childrensgriefawarenessday.org
2. Dowdney, 2000: Haine, et al., 2008, www.childrensgriefawarenessday.org
3. *Grieving in Schools: Nationwide Survey among Classroom Teachers on Childhood Bereavement*—conducted by New York Life Foundation and American Federation of Teachers, 2012, www.childrensgriefawarenessday.org
4. "The Lord is near to the brokenhearted and saves the crushed in spirit." Psalm 34:18. "Keep your heart with all vigilance, for from it flow the springs of life." Proverbs 4:23
5. Wolfelt, 1996
6. Karen Lindwall-Bourg & Geraldine Haggard, *Strength for the Journey: Help for the Whole Family in the Shadow of Grief and Mourning, 2011*—with gratitude to Mark Hundley!
7. God is sad over the sinfulness of men, Genesis 6:6-8. His Spirit is grieved over the disobedience of the church, Isaiah 63:10 & Ephesians 4:30. And Jesus is even called the "Man of sorrows" who is very familiar (acquainted) with grief, Isaiah 53:3-10; Matthew 23:37-39; Luke 13:34-35; & John 11:35

8. A God who creates us with such intricate uniquenesses and counts every hair on our heads and knows the number of our days and provided his Son to die on the cross for us and loves us more immensely and completely than is humanly comprehendible and more, understands both the sameness of grief and the uniqueness of grief. "Are not two sparrows sold for a penny? And not one of them will fall to the ground apart from your Father. But even the hairs of your head are all numbered. Fear not, therefore; you are of more value than many sparrows." Matthew 10:29-31. "For you formed my inward parts; you knitted me together in my mother's womb. I praise you, for I am fearfully and wonderfully made. Wonderful are your works; my soul knows it very well. Your eyes saw my unformed substance; in your book were written, every one of them, the days that were formed for me, when as yet there was none of them." Psalm 139:13-14, 16

www.ingramcontent.com/pod-product-compliance
Lightning Source LLC
Chambersburg PA
CBHW070553300426
44113CB00011B/1895